DISAPPOINTING ALICE

Rachel Piercey

HAPPENSTANCE

BY THE SAME AUTHOR:
Rivers Wanted (The Emma Press, 2014)
The Flower and the Plough (The Emma Press, 2013)

ACKNOWLEDGMENTS:
'Hwæt' is collaged from translations of the first word of *Beowulf*, including
several of my own.

My gratitude to the editors of *Ash, Butcher's Dog, The Interpreter's House, The
Poetry Review, The Rialto, The Scores* and *The Tangerine*, where several of these
poems (or earlier versions) first appeared, and to the judges of the *Magma,
Poetry London* and *Troubadour* competitions for commending some of them.

Thank you to my mum, dad, sister and brother-in-law for their love and
support; to Will for always understanding and inspiring me; and to Anna
Kirk, James Trevelyan, Kayo Chingonyi, Sophie Baker, Ruth Wiggins,
Jacqueline Saphra, John Canfield, John Clegg, Emily Hasler, Maurice Riordan,
Mike Sims and Emma Wright for their poetic friendship and encouragement.
Particular thanks to the brilliant and generous Kathryn Maris, who has
helped so many of these poems find their best form.

Neither the pamphlet title nor the title poem refer to any of my lovely
real-life Alices.

Printed by The Dolphin Press
www.dolphinpress.co.uk

First published in 2019 by HappenStance Press,
21 Hatton Green, Glenrothes, Fife KY7 4SD
nell@happenstancepress.com
www.happenstancepress.com

CONTENTS

For my wonderful Will

HWÆT

Well · Hey · Come · Mark me
Hark · See · So

Right · Hear me · Let's get started
Here · Oi · Lo

Legend says · The story goes
We know · Behold · There once was

Listen · Look · I'll tell you this
The world · is full · of monsters

SONG FOR AMELIA

Come in, Amelia, this is the Canary.
My singing soul is my open circuit
and how I need your flick-fire to complete it.
I know I only have you for a while.

Come in, Yellow Peril, this is the Canary.
We must rise above our jealousies
and accept the function of our lives.
By wing or wheel, let her drive us wild.

Come in, Friendship, this is the Canary.
Roar with our forward-thrust—
change is history's role for us;
we are skilled at shifting heaviness.

Come in, Avian, this is the Canary.
We must be all lung. How often
my radial ruff of cylinders
has heaved for air! We are the lucky ones.

Come in, Pitcairn, this is the Canary.
However tinny, let us sing
our love for her: how she prefers
the air thin, the horizon undulating.

Come in, Vega, this is the Canary.
What fuel for our clicking brains,
the cogs of etymology
in her name! What a perfect thrum!

Come in, Electra, this is the Canary.
How many things, between us,
we've made better. Come in, Electra.
Come in, Electra. Come in, Electra.

Note: The Canary was Amelia Earhart's first plane. Friend-
ship, Avian, Pitcairn, Vega and Electra were all aircraft flown
by her. Yellow Peril was her Kissel Speedster car.

SPRING CLEANING

Sometimes when I am hauling
the hoover round the house
I get to feeling a little dangerous
and tug on its stretchy neck
without caring to check the trajectory
of its small hot body. I would be frightened
to feed a horse with apples
but I feed the hoover dusty hairballs
and do not flinch from its bristly nuzzle
and emphatic swallow. At all times
I keep my eye trained on the hoover
to enjoy its vanishing of lumps
but I must blink
and a robin keeps arriving in the garden
and my first crocus is exerting itself
through the soil and it is always in these moments
that it happens—the tangible rattle
up the hose of something substantial,
which might matter, which might be
something I wouldn't want to lose,
stuck now in a matted shroud,
and I could go searching for it
but that would allow everything out.

LOST KEY

As with a pole he guides his craft, tends sail,
And in the black boat ferries o'er his dead ...
 —Aeneid, Book VI, trans. Theodore C. Williams

You have to trust
   the locksmith,

   the one who comes in the night
with his box of tricks.

   It sticks in your throat
as he coaxes the lock,

how such a trivial loss
   can mean this threshold
      is not yours.

Look how the locksmith
   is calmly captaining the door,

   how soon, for him,
the mechanism moves.

   He stands aside.

Take the coins from your eyes
   and pass through.

BAD APPLE

And if we all possess   at least one bad apple
in the barrel of ourselves,   is it not better for it to settle
at the top, where the rot   may be easily perceived
and so scooped out?   Thus mused she,
and he, who believed   her comely barrel-ful
to be tight-celled and stain-free,   felt most sorrowful.
How she took pleasure   in the contagious mush,
she liked to nudge it with her finger.   She thought she would love
to go further,   to slough off the heavy lid
and let the apples scatter,   for the thrill that they might trip.

KATE BUSH AS SPIDER GODDESS

You are fourteen and learning who to worship.
You are learning about stars,
French verbs and oxbow lakes and
(though you couldn't put it into words)
the roles that history makes for you.
The options are sticking in your soul like flies.
You are learning to negotiate
the things you want, and what other people think

and from the chaos comes Kate.
And Kate calmly sinks her spider-jaws
into *chaste* and *whore* and feasts on *witch*
and from the meat of them
spins a text with the kick of steel.
And Kate's many eyes look right through *never*
and if you gaze at Kate
you find you are the whole story
and if you gaze at Kate then your body
and mind get red and hot and swap themselves
and reconcile. You dream in Kate.
Kate can tell you about love and Kate knows
that the lightest things—like air, like snow—
can hold the truth. And between Kate's various limbs
beats a lion's heart. And Kate is hard
and high as adulthood. And you are fourteen
and you are scared of spiders.
But you are learning.
Let her inside. Let her spin.

DEEP IN THE DESERT

Alice was a disappointer
of people she loved and who loved her.
These people loved her deeply,
though the topsoil of their affection was thinning.
Her interactions felt crumbly.

Alice sent a message re. her total dereliction
of spirit and body in a far-off country,
stripped of wallet and phone.

Please come, I am deep in the desert,
I am where the gold
shades into the bone, please come,
and we can catch up while you're at it.

They all felt terse and arid
about disappointing Alice.

CHIVALRY STREET

This is the sword hour, and this the lute.
These are the slim necks of pennants
and these the women, hair loose to their waists.
This is everyone knowing their place.
These are the men, bound for heaven.
This is reeking blood and this the song
for the breath of women, which is sweet.
These are the women not breathing.
This is them being loved, a knight apiece.
These are the rules. This is a poem
which expresses them; this is a revivalist painting.
These are the women with their hair long.
This is a seductive uncomplication.
This is the modern woman, whose symbolisms compete,
and this is her considering Chivalry Street.
This is her lock of token-ready hair
and this her pliable handkerchief.

GAME

Guess Who?—The Classic Mystery Face Game.
Is your person wearing a hat? Does your person have blue eyes?

Neatly, we wait for the resurrection.
We didn't always call it that—

at first we didn't even know our names.
We lay cool and calm in our tray

of absolute darkness.
Then came the first shake

and the rattling upright. The light
was very bright in our wide eyes.

That time, we learnt Paul and Anita and Sarah,
hair colour, glasses and hats.

When we were flicked back and boxed up
the darkness seemed thicker.

Gradually we came to know ourselves better.
Some of us liked the sick clack

of being swung upwards,
others the sleekness of oily thumbs.

We shared words for the bitterness
of the game being done,

of being slung flat and packed away
for another monotony of months.

We sang useless lullabies from our hard blue beds
to our counterparts in red—

we didn't know what to call them
and we didn't know what to say to Hans

when the other Hans slipped away.
Each time we are lifted from the shelf

he grows sadder. We start to talk
about souls and the unfamiliarity of age.

We parse over and over
the toppling intensity of the wait.

POST-FILM,

he has the pleasant sense of being watched.
The cameras are trained on his back
as he walks naturally towards the gents,
opening the door in a manner
which implies upper-body strength.
The way to describe what he is doing
is *pissing*, or maybe *taking a slash*.
Even the way he washes his hands is interesting,
half slapdash, peering casually in the mirror,
half attending to the build-up of germs.
It suggests just the occasional rearing of nerves.
From this angle, all the girls in his past
are beautiful, sunlit and melancholic,
and all the girls in his future are beautiful
and sunlit too. And every mistake
is softened and understandable. And even the rain
on his face will be the applauding of hands.

GLASS SLIPPER

The Prince is charming
and we take the word
to have no edge.

Everyone's character
is reliably manifest.
Cinderella makes appallingly

light work of goodness.
If a man and his father's army
pursued me down

a flight of steps—
even into the softest darkness
and however profuse the stars—

I would scream until my voice
smashed, and find another use
for my heels of glass.

This isn't why I'm weeping.
Cinderella tells the Prince
she loves him

and he has always loved her
and the glass slipper
is just a glittering metaphor

and it should mean little
or even nothing,
and it shouldn't mean everything.

COMPLAINT

My lord has sent for Capability.
He is tired of my jewelled knot gardens
and low, tessellating hedges.
Estates are Grecian now,
all graceful lines,
grass like a falling dress
and cool white masonry to rest the eyes.
Goodbye, Versailles!
Though in my grounds he enjoys
certain aspects of the sublime,
he has set follies on my fingers
and all my prohibitive edges are disguised.

RICHMOND PARK PASTORALISES
RACHEL PIERCEY

Come live with us and be our love

and we will ripely misunderstand you
who are human pleasures' proof
mobile in neon Lycra

your sense of time so linear   petite
your body yours
your rosy dreams   and sleep

to have words to say   exactly
how you feel
how you grow
O Rachel come
to our sweet bower of loam

though
should you prefer it edgy   we invoke
our liminality   the city
nuzzling heath   your ambiguity

unflowering actions   root-bound morals
wadding your anxious heart
down into poems

O Rachel
we tire of leisure   we want
your tantalising
melancholy
terror

MYCORRHIZA

With the fungus,
I am an honoured guest.
The fungus fits my tongue
and secretes its threads.

The fungus says,
You are using us.
We will need to drink your sugars.

ABOUT THE RIVER

'...he says you could not step twice into the same river...'
—Heraclitus, according to Plato

I asked the lonely stretch of river
to tell me more about my lover;
he loved this place when he was younger.

The river hunched its chilly shoulder:
Remember the one about the river?
The water here is not his water.
The water's always flowing further
and can't be said to be the river.

I tried again and asked the water
about the banks my love leaned over
which made the rearing waves declare:
Do not define me by my borders!
A lake might give such easy answers
but only the sea has the mouth of the river.

I bent towards the deepest boulders
and asked if they could make him clearer
but the bed blew clouds into the water:
The things that build up under here
are solely for the river's ears.

So I asked my lover about the river
he pitched and skimmed and floated over,
but looking round I found him nowhere:
remember the one about the lover?

THE SEA OF MARRIAGEABILITY

When I went to the sea of marriageability
I took a costly offering, naturally.

I ripped off every pretty stitch of cloth
and waded in. The water was butter-soft;

I had to stand on tippy-toes to breathe.
Give me give me give me said the sea.

I will give you every single thing I own,
I answer-prayed, *for a retroussé nose.*

In the wavy heat, my salt-flecked freckles
glistened like meat on heaving tables.

The sea would see what it had got for me.
But first, it swallowed my offering.

MY SISTER

After the stories of Mary and Martha, Luke 10:38-42 and John 12:1-8

In quiet moments, we uncover the jar.
Now nothing moves my heart
like the scent of spikenard;

it treasures the air like his name
which we save up to say.
But I think she is shamed

by the way they told our story.
That day, I was a free wheel
and she was stuck with heat

but neither of us is so anchored
in a simple character.
Another mood's Martha

would have dropped at his feet
and wound them with oiled sheets
of her hair, musk-sweet.

We slip the cloth from the jar
and breathe the heavy gold air.
He knew all this, I tell my sister.

FIVE GO TO THE ISLAND AGAIN

Timmy is long dead, and the others scattered.
Like picnic crumbs, thinks Anne

on those occasional sweetly devastating days
when there's a gust of island air,

coast-cupped, hot and sandy
and with no place here in Hertfordshire,

where her daughter is darting out of school
with the news that she will play Miranda.

The heroine! Claire is so full of stardom
she lets Anne lean in to kiss her hair

which smells of Kirrin, which smells
of salt and ginger and sweat,

manageable space and independence.
Anne doesn't care for Ferdinand

or Prospero, but when she says as much,
her daughter flounces off.

I might call him / A thing divine
says Miranda, who has never seen a young man,

and Anne thinks of wilful Claire,
who would rather toss her head and swear

and get herself the hell out,
or Ferdinand out, or whatever suited her,

and how Anne admires her—
though on opening night it is clear

that the girl is no actor,
has to fight to call the teenage boys *Sir*

and Anne imagines herself up there
among the crepe-paper fronds of seaweed

and the cardboard palm trees
and there again is that island air,

warmth and grit, cowslip, wild garlic,
and now here's something rich and strange—

Miranda is going to stay,
she will not be Queen of Naples

so she waves off the boat of lordly men
and she sinks into the rough sand

with Ariel and Caliban, and they start again.

O CAPTAINS

I love all captains   their voices calmly crackling
on the tannoy   thanking us   for travelling
        for our seatedness
        for not making a fuss
as we are rumbled   glinting   off the earth
    and back again
                                and most of all
    I love captains
                            who are carrying   me home
    who have manipulated the air
                        to bear me   over
                Land's End or Dover
                                nosing through clouds
to the soft green   revelation underneath them
down   down   down
        O captains
striding capably
        through the airport's
    blank caverns   straightening   your decorated
            hats   wheeling your small
square bags
                    may you always sleep deeply
                            eat cleanly
                        maintain your honest
        open faces
    and know to take each of us
            back to our best place

I DIED IN THE ARCHERS

but the women were marvellous.
They discussed it for weeks,
and it was a sharp pleasure
hearing their praise of me
without confronting the brute
bruise of my body. Now each tongue
bears my pall and renders me
ex-physical. Eulogise me, Lynda,
with the gold wine of the canon.
Sluice it, Susan, through the town.
Kate, burn sage, to waft my spirit on.

LOVE

Because it can see for two miles,
I have set a peacock on the roof.

Certain folk it regards as friends,
and then it hurries down to strut

around the dusty moat of yard
and make a revelation of its tail,

or simply does not pause in prising
insects from the slatted wood.

In many ways it is well-trained.
I mean, it is trained in many ways

by a variety of guests,
so it is tactically efficient.

Take this shape on the horizon:
slow, resolving, barrelling

into sight, towards the fence,
and how the peacock tenses, trembles,

starts to strike out with its claws,
and how it crashes through the yard

to scream at the stranger, gaining fast.
I'm contemplating something bad.

I have one hand upon the latch.
I have one hand upon the axe.